What is ear wax?
Made inside your ears, ear wax catches dust
and dirt that flies in. The wax creeps out and
your ears stay clean!

Step inside...

Contents

Did you know you blink
about 10,000 times every day?

2

What are tears?
Tears are the water your eyes produce all the time. They keep your eyes nice and clean by washing them whenever you blink.

...and learn about
Your body

Did you know you lose and replace about 90 hairs a day?

I know what my body is!

I know what my body looks like because I can see it in the **mirror**. But what does my body do?

we grow **taller** **until** we become adults

we le**arn** **to** **walk**

we le**arn** **to talk**

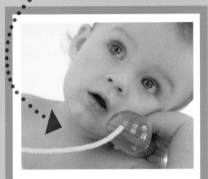

Baby time

Your body is working hard from the moment you are born. Babies are growing all the time and learning about the world around them.

Toddler time

As you grow up you start to look different from other people – often having different-coloured hair, eyes, or skin than your friends.

Growing up

You carry on growing for about 18-20 years – that's a long time! Measure your height regularly to see how quickly you grow.

On the outside we all look different.
But on the inside we all work the same.

5

I'm a girl

What's outside?

blond

We all look different on the **outside**. From the colour of our eyes and skin, to the **colour** and length of our hair.

Skin

Your body is covered in skin. Skin is like a big bag that keeps everything inside.

my skin

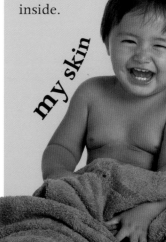

Skin is waterproof – it doesn't let any water into our bodies.

6

Muscles

Your body has muscles everywhere. They are the things that help you to move.

you have over 600 muscles

look!

Your face and neck have 30 muscles. How many faces can you pull?

9

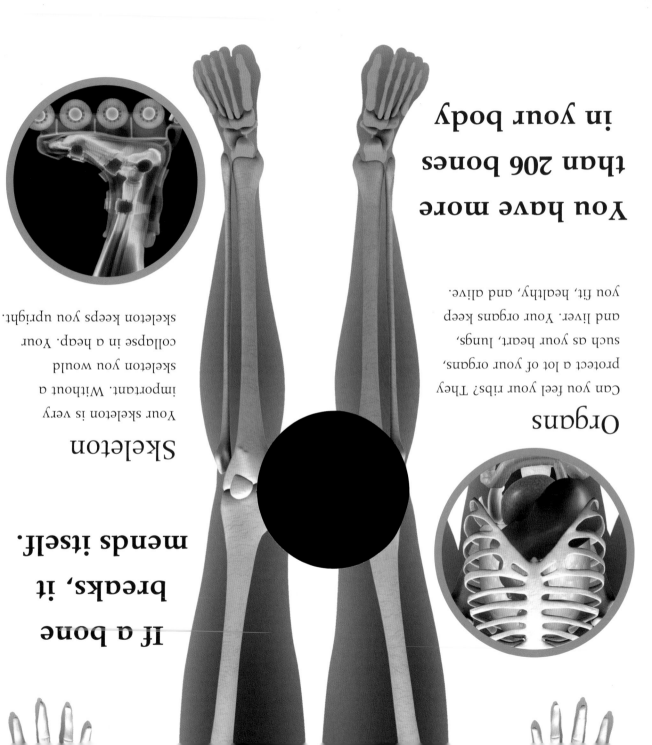

You have more than 206 bones in your body

Organs

Can you feel your ribs? They protect a lot of your organs, such as your heart, lungs, and liver. Your organs keep you fit, healthy, and alive.

Skeleton

Your skeleton is very important. Without a skeleton you would collapse in a heap. Your skeleton keeps you upright.

If a bone breaks, it mends itself.

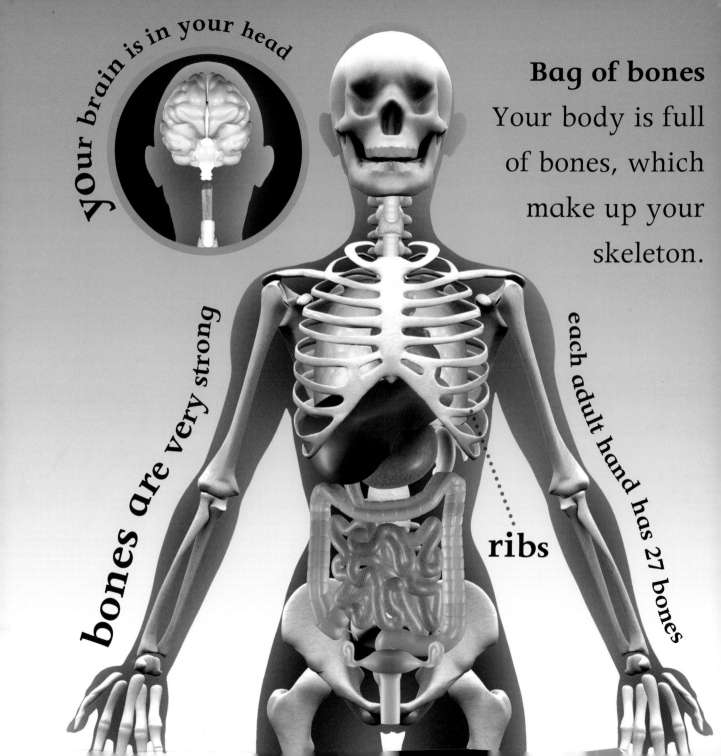

your brain is in your head

Bag of bones
Your body is full
of bones, which
make up your
skeleton.

bones are very strong

each adult hand has 27 bones

ribs

Let's go...

Think of all the things you do in a day –
running, jumping, **playing**, eating,
talking. Your body works really hard
when you're awake.

Exercise is good for you – and it's fun, too!

Body doctor

let me take a look

am I ill?

...let's stop

After a busy day your body needs to **rest**, so it's very important to get plenty of  **sleep**. When you're tired you might start to yawn.

What is a yawn?

Everybody yawns – even animals. But no-one knows for sure why we do it. Some people think it gives us a big extra breath when we're tired.

Brainbox

Everything you do, from drinking a glass of water to jumping over a puddle is controlled by your **brain**. It's just like a computer, but more clever.

look at my brain!

Where is your brain?

Knock on your head, it's hard isn't it? That hard bone is called your skull and underneath it is your soft brain. Your skull protects your brain from bumps.

Your brain works all the time – even when you are fast asleep.

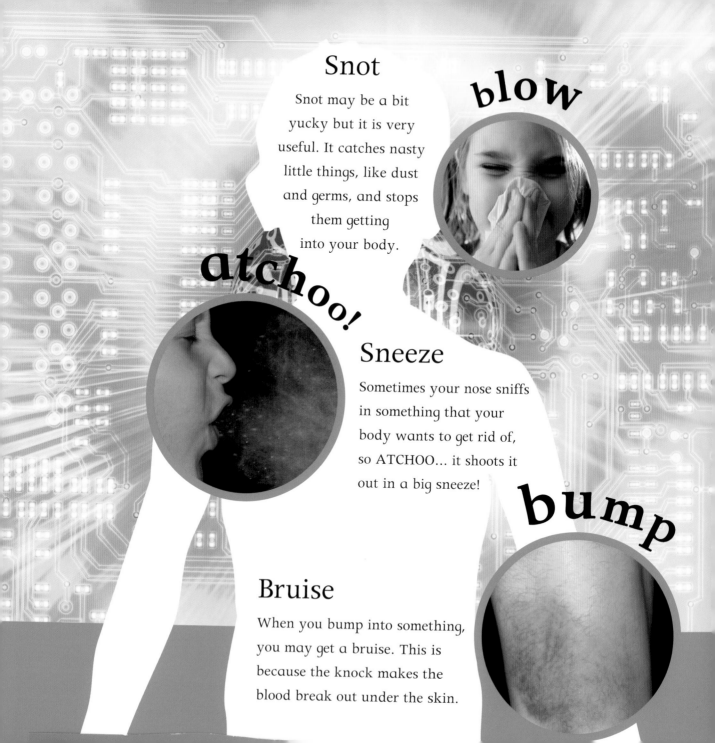

Snot

Snot may be a bit yucky but it is very useful. It catches nasty little things, like dust and germs, and stops them getting into your body.

blow

atchoo!

Sneeze

Sometimes your nose sniffs in something that your body wants to get rid of, so ATCHOO... it shoots it out in a big sneeze!

bump

Bruise

When you bump into something, you may get a bruise. This is because the knock makes the blood break out under the skin.

My body makes me better!

I've got a cold

Your body gets rid of colds all by itself – the coughs and sneezes are actually making you better.

Staying well

We need injections to keep away really bad illnesses. They only take a moment and they keep us healthy.

bohydrates

bread, potatoes, and rice give you energy.

Cuts

When you graze your knee, your blood springs into action. It rushes there taking special things called platelets with it, which make a scab. The scab protects the cut.

My blood fixes my cuts

Ouch!

Sight
Your eyes see and tell your brain what something looks like.

Senses

Your senses tell your brain if something is good to eat, safe to touch, and lots, lots more. Your senses are...

Taste
Your tongue tastes and tells your brain if something is good or horrible to eat.

Smell
Your nose tells your brain whether something smells nice or nasty.

Hearing
Your ears tell your brain what things sound like.

13

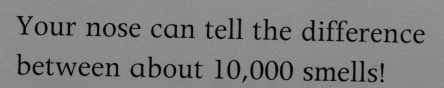

Your nose can tell the difference between about 10,000 smells!

Touch test

All of our senses work together to give us a big message.
Take away your sense of sight and see if you can tell what
things are just by touching them. It's harder than you think!

Touch

Your body,
particularly your
hands, tells your
brain what things
feel like.

Take four bowls and put
four different things in
them, examples below.

Blindfold your friends
and ask them what is in
each bowl by making
them feel it.

feel my soft cuddly toy

Examples

A peeled grape
A cold, cooked sausage
Slightly wet, cold spaghetti
A lump of modelling clay
An egg - but be careful!
Blocks of ice

Can they guess what they're touching?

You **see** an apple, it looks good to eat.

You **feel** with your fingers that it is smooth and hard.

When you see an apple, your nose, eyes, ears, fingers, and mouth send messages to your brain to tell you if it's good to eat. These are called your **senses**.

It **smells** fresh when you pick it up

You **hear** a nice crunch when you bite into it.

It **tastes** delicious.

15

Body talk

How do you tell someone if you are **happy** or sad? You talk to them of course. But there are other ways to talk too.

> **How are you? Are you happy or sad?**

> I'm **happy**!

 You use your tongue, lips, and teeth to change sounds into words – that's talking.

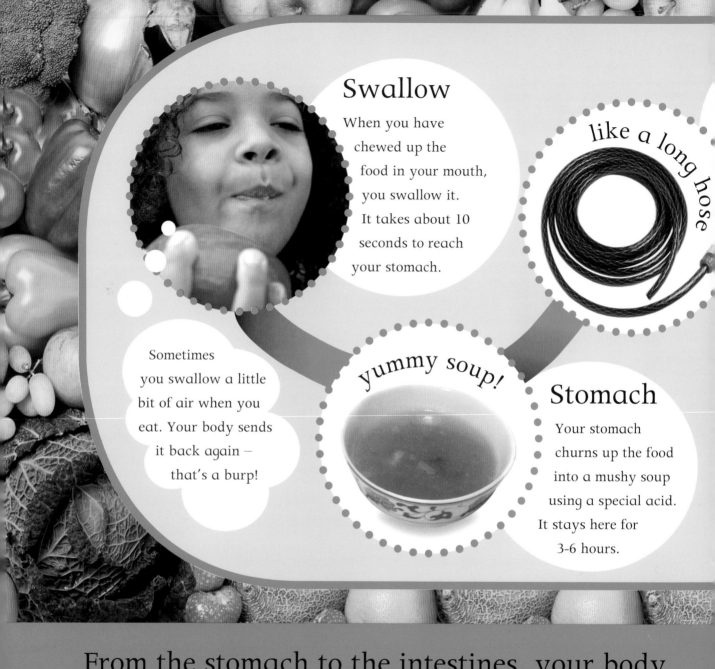

Swallow

When you have chewed up the food in your mouth, you swallow it. It takes about 10 seconds to reach your stomach.

like a long hose

Sometimes you swallow a little bit of air when you eat. Your body sends it back again – that's a burp!

Yummy soup!

Stomach

Your stomach churns up the food into a mushy soup using a special acid. It stays here for 3-6 hours.

From the stomach to the intestines, your body takes out all the goodness from your food.

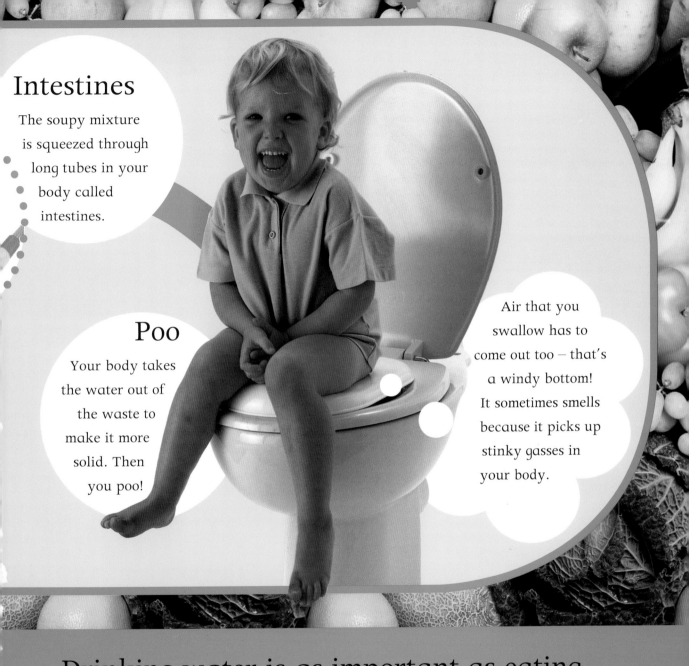

Intestines

The soupy mixture is squeezed through long tubes in your body called intestines.

Poo

Your body takes the water out of the waste to make it more solid. Then you poo!

Air that you swallow has to come out too – that's a windy bottom! It sometimes smells because it picks up stinky gasses in your body.

Drinking water is as important as eating food. Water makes your blood flow well.

Eat up!

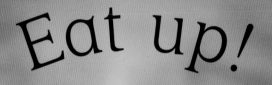

Have you ever wondered
what happens to your food
when you've **swallowed**
it? It goes on a long journey.